The State Bed in the Lord
Chancellor's room at Wimpole Hall,
Cambridgeshire

# A Guide to England
## *Through a Cat's Eyes*

# A Guide to England
# *Through a Cat's Eyes*

## Pat Albeck

William Morrow and Company, Inc.
New York

It is the policy of William Morrow and Company, Inc., and its
imprints and affiliates, recognizing the importance of preserving
what has been written, to print the books we publish on acid-free
paper, and we exert our best efforts to that end.

Library of Congress Cataloging-in-Publication Data

Albeck,Pat.
    A guide to England through a cat's eyes/ Pat Albeck.
        p.   cm.
    ISBN 0-688-12341-4
    1. Cats—Humor. 2. Pets and travel—Humor. 3. England—
    Description and travel—Humor.   I. Title.
    PN6231.C23A43   1993
914.204-859-0207—dc20                          93-1325
                                                   CIP


Printed in the United States of America

First Edition

1 2 3 4 5 6 7 8 9 10

Book Design by Brian Sisco

for

*Elizabeth and Kitty*

# *Acknowledgments*

The author would like to thank the following
people for their help:

Liz and John Bonython
Emma Bridgewater
Lady Cave
Sheila and Terri Chetham
Warren Davis
Ray Hallett
Kate Harris
Rhonda McNicol
Penny Phillips
Candida Stewart-Sandeman
Matthew Rice
Peter Rice
Douglas and Mary Anne Schwalbe
and
Martin Pumphry for driving me round
Cornwall on top of his fish van
Special thanks to my editor, Will Schwalbe,
whose idea it was to do a book,
and
Michael Alcock,
Kate Hill, and Wanda Whiteley
at
Boxtree

I LIVE IN WEST LONDON. Many London cats spend all their lives between the window, the front door, and the garden wall, with the occasional nighttime wander over the rooftops; I am lucky enough to be able to travel.

The humans with whom I live do not trust me to stay at home for long without them. They can't keep me locked in the house because of the canary. And there are goldfish at the bottom of the garden. Of course, when they visit places in London they needn't take me, but I go just the same. I go wandering alone too, along the river to visit local friends. I go to some of the extremely good local pubs: The Black Lion, The Dove, The Old Ship, The Blue Anchor, and The Rutland, where there is sometimes the chance of leftovers. I like to walk along the river toward Hammersmith Bridge, but only when there aren't too many dogs being walked. There are two dogs in my house, who are extremely friendly and courteous, but strange dogs have a tendency to chase me, so I avoid them whenever possible. There are cats who live on the houseboats along the river, and people live there too. If I sit on the wall I can see sailing boats and police tugs.

On SUMMER EVENINGS, FROM MY FRONT GARDEN, I can hear the music and see the lights from the pleasure steamers.

Going west along the river there are exciting things to see: swans, geese, herons, and cormorants. When the tide is low I wander across the shingle to the Eyot, a small island, where I once found a water rat.

London is full of wildlife. Last summer a seal was seen near the Eyot. Foxes are not an unusual sight around here, and they go even farther into London, to see what they can find in the dustbins.

Some of the houses along Chiswick Mall are very imposing. There is a resident black cat who constantly crosses the road to make people feel they are going to be lucky. Black cats crossing paths is a lucky sign in England. At the end of Chiswick Mall is the Church of St. Nicholas. I go through the graveyard where Hogarth is buried. His painting of *The Graham Children*, which is in the Tate Gallery, includes a tabby cat looking rather fiercely at a goldfinch. I slip through a path by the side of the graveyard, across the road into Chiswick House.

DESIGNED BY LORD BURLINGTON IN 1727, Chiswick
House was built in the style of Palladio. It is set in the most beautiful
park. There is a lake inhabited by all kinds of ducks and geese, moorhens
and coots, and a heron; in the trees around the lake there is even a flock
of parakeets.

The formal paths are lined with statues, urns, and sphinxes, and are punctuated with temples and obelisks. It is a favorite place for humans to walk their well-behaved dogs and children. There are trees to climb, and blackberries and chestnuts to collect. Not many cats visit here, but I like to look at statues of my lion relations. I feel the sphinxes are possibly cousins once removed.

Two of my favorite pastimes are eating and shopping. I especially like shopping for things to eat. One of the most famous stores in London is Harrods. Everyone I know goes there to see the fish department. Each day a different display of fresh fish is arranged; the smells are almost too much for a cat to bear. If I manage to take my eyes off the fish and look up to the ceiling, I can gaze at a series of tiles depicting hunting and sporting scenes. They were designed by W. J. Neatby and made by Royal Doulton in 1902. I spend a great deal of time down in the food halls, but I also like to go to the pet department on the second floor, where there is a good selection of tinned delicacies for cats.

On the way to the book department, full of intriguing books on cats, I always stop to look at the television sets. Seeing thirty large, twenty small, and twenty tiny images of a wildlife program about unusual rodents is quite a good way to spend half an hour or so.

15

Not far from Harrods is one of my favorite buildings in London. Designed about 1910 for the Michelin tire company, it now houses the Conran shop, an excellent place to buy furniture, china, glass, linen, toys, and food, and all kinds of presents. Upstairs there is a restaurant called Bibendum. Downstairs in the doorway is an oyster bar; outside, fish and flowers are sold.

17

I PARTICULARLY LIKE WANDERING DOWN the King's Road in Chelsea, although there are not too many cats strolling along because the traffic is so heavy. The shops sell trendy clothes, food, shoes, and books; there are also cafés, restaurants, and antiques markets. The humans are interesting too: serious clothes shoppers, antiques collectors, eccentrics, locals buying provisions, all looking at each other or being looked at.

Sometimes I wander off into the side streets, where some of my richer friends live. North toward the Fulham and Brompton roads are some very pretty and very grand houses. One of my friends, who lives in The Boltons, tells me he gets quite a lot of smoked salmon. The best time to walk around is spring, when the bulbs, blossoms, and cats come out. In Chelsea there seems to be a cat in every window, door, gateway, and cellar.

If I turn south off the King's Road toward the river, I come to the Royal Hospital, home of the Chelsea Pensioners. The building was designed by Christopher Wren in the seventeenth century. Every May the grounds are taken over by the Royal Horticultural Society for the Chelsea Flower Show: five glorious days when gardeners and people who love flowers come to look at the new varieties of roses, the latest ideas in garden arrangements, and maybe a bird table or a fishpond. People discuss the plants with great seriousness, sometimes talking about them as if they were people: "Where could we put her?"

"I hear she does quite well on a north wall." There is talk in every language—people come to exhibit and visit from all over the world. And it is one of the few places where people seem to be talking in Latin. How is a cat expected to know that *Nepeta gigantea* is catmint? On the last day, when the flowers on show are sold, people can be seen walking to the Underground with tall delphiniums or lilies way above their heads.

24

I HAVE NEVER MANAGED TO GET INTO a London theater—but I like to walk in "Theaterland" and see the lights. One theater has Cats written above it; maybe they'll let me in there. What could *"The Mousetrap* running for forty years" mean? I like to turn into Rupert Street [see the previous page] to see the fruit and vegetables on the market stalls. The cats living here visit the local Italian food shops for treats. A short stroll from Shaftesbury Avenue brings me to Covent Garden, home of the Royal Opera House, Bow Street Police Station, and what used to be the fruit and flower market. There are so many shops and cafés, and so many people, it is easy to get caught underfoot.

A LARGE PART OF MY TIME IS SPENT on rooftops and high walls and up in trees, but the things I usually prefer to look at are quite near the ground. Some of the most beautiful elements of church decoration, for example, are to be found on the floors. I tend to concentrate on these while the humans look up at columns, capitals, windows, and ceilings.

The first signs of the remains of the Roman Palace at Fishbourne were found by archaeologists in 1961, and for the next seven years much excavation was carried out. Traces of structures going back to the time of the Roman invasion of Britain at the beginning of the first century were uncovered. From the layout of the floors, some of which are very well preserved, the whole site can be imagined.

There is one second-century mosaic floor in remarkable condition, depicting a dolphin, sea panthers, and sea horses. There are interesting patterns to be seen on the ground in a lot of places I visit. I am very keen on the huge black-and-white flagstones in the hall at Dyrham Park. The tiles on the floor of the Church of All Saints, Margaret Street, are magnificent. And I have sneaked into a London club or two and found the most amazing floors. It is difficult for humans to sneak into private clubs, but cats can: The floor of the Reform Club in Pall Mall is well worth a look. The Victorians and Edwardians were very keen on tiling entrance halls, doorways, and garden paths. The patterns and colors are very simple: yellow ocher, terra-cotta, blue, white, and black. I do love Victorian and Edwardian tiled hallways and doorways.

I am quite interested in the patterns on carpets too, but the temptation to scratch up the pile stops me from inspecting too many.

Saying good-bye to home and one's friends is always hard, however exciting the prospects of a journey, but once on the road I become very happy. Because I don't drive myself, I can't really choose where I want to go, but I make it very clear when I am pleased or displeased about our direction. I like to take a lot of time to get where we're going. It is the going, not the arriving, I like. There are so many attractive-looking names on the signposts, animals and flowers to sniff, things to eat. I think we should be able to stop whenever the fancy takes us. Even if we don't wander off main roads there are still glorious things to see: kestrels hovering, fields of cows, farms with interesting build-ings—surely full of happy farm cats longing for a visit.

There are unexpected color combinations everywhere. It is no surprise now to find brilliant acid-yellow fields outnumbering the green meadows. These yellow fields are filled with rape grown to make rape-seed oil. Bluish-green fields of spring cabbages mix with the grayer blue-green leeks and yellower green lettuce. Later in the year *everything* turns golden.

The fields are so much bigger than they used to be. An awful lot

of hedges have gone. Apart from making the landscape less interesting, this means there are fewer places for birds and small animals, fewer flowers, and fewer haunts for a cat. Of course there are rabbits and mice in the fields before harvesting takes place, but where can they run to when the cover has gone? Luckily, much of the English countryside is cared for by people who like to shoot game birds: If they didn't, we would have no hedges, no small woods or copses.

"A day away from Chartwell is a day wasted."
—Winston Churchill

CHARTWELL, NOW OWNED BY THE NATIONAL TRUST, was the home of Sir Winston Churchill. When I visit the house I can really believe he is still alive. His studio is full of his painting materials. There are collections of cigars and walking sticks, uniforms, medals, and hats. There is the chair where he used to sit alone with his ginger cat, Jock, watching goldfish and thinking and planning. There is a rose garden filled with yellow and gold roses, which their children gave to the Churchills as a present for their Golden Wedding.

Sir Winston loved animals and they loved him. One of his geese always followed him as he took a walk in the garden. A robin would come and feed from his hand. And he had two poodles as pets, as well as the famous Jock. The original Jock died in 1976, but there is always a marmalade cat living at Chartwell. The house wouldn't look the same without one. If I were a marmalade cat, I might have applied to live at Chartwell. But a nice marmalade kitten passed his "audition" quite recently and tells me he is very happy there.

M OTTISFONT ABBEY HAS THE MOST COMPREHENSIVE COLLECTION of roses in the country. In May and June it is probably the sweetest-smelling place in England. It is open from April to October and is run by the National Trust.

The nicest thing about the rose gardens is the way the roses are planted with other flowers: cream and white foxgloves, campanula and yellow irises. It is not only the mixture of colors that is so pleasing but also the different shapes and textures one gets with this kind of planting. Some of the beds are edged with aquilegia, wild geraniums, pinks, lavender, and catmint. Some of the climbing roses grow over arches and pergolas or trail through ancient fruit trees.

There are many perpetually flowering roses among Mottisfont's collection. Favorite roses of mine are Canary Bird, Goldfinch, and Little White Pet.

The Names of the Roses:

*Opposite page, top:* Louise Odier

   *Opposite page, bottom:* Rosa Mundi

      *This page, top:* Tuscany

        *This page, bottom:* Constance Spry

INTO KENT, FAMOUS FOR HOPS AND FRUIT. I don't know
whether I prefer it in spring, when everything is covered in blossom, early
summer, when cherries and strawberries are cropped, or late summer,
when the apples and pears begin to ripen.

I TAKE MY MOST FREQUENT JOURNEYS INTO the English country-side in the late summer and autumn because there are so many treats to find. Stansted Park is a lovely country house, set in a beautiful park and woodlands, on the Sussex-Hampshire border. It is privately owned and open to the public on weekends. The house was destroyed by fire in the eighteenth century and was rebuilt in the 1920s.

The original stable block still exists, and also this charming private chapel. There is a lot of food to be found in the woods and fields. The best blackberries seem to grow here.

There are also lovely mushrooms: I wish I liked them more. This time of year I go for lots of walks in the fields and woods. Where the two meet is the best place for finding food and the best place for picnics. (Please see the next picture of me, with a friend, after a feast.)

SELBORNE WAS THE HOME OF GILBERT WHITE, who, like me, was extremely interested in birds (and other wildlife). Like most people, he could never figure out why cats like fish so much—yet don't like swimming or getting wet. I don't know myself, but maybe we all like food that is out of reach. Gilbert White wrote *The Natural History of*

*Selborne*, a diary of country happenings. It amazes me that he didn't think swallows, swifts, and other summer visiting birds migrated in the winter. He thought they hibernated. I often look around to see if I can see a dormant swallow or swift just in case he was right: He wasn't, and I think he finally realized this too.

41

I AM ALWAYS TEMPTED WHENEVER I SEE SIGNS on the
road advertising something. Food sold by the roadside is cheaper,
fresher, and better.

People who leave produce for sale outside their garden gates are so trusting. They place a tin for money alongside and expect you to take the right number of apples or beets and leave the right change. Because the things are such a bargain, I always buy much more food than I need.

The main attractions for a cat are other cats and food. And where there is food there are usually other cats.

CATS ARE NOT ENCOURAGED TO TAKE PART IN ball games. The balls are either too large or too hard. I like to watch ball games anyway. Humans seem to like watching too: There are always huge crowds at soccer games and cricket matches. A favorite English pastime is to sit on the village green on a hot summer afternoon and listen to the

sound of leather on willow. There are many claims as to where the game was first played. But the basic rules were established in 1775 by the landlord of Hambledon's Bat and Ball Inn. The original public house and Hambledon club cricket ground are one and a half miles from the beautiful Georgian village of Hambledon.

Outdoor events change the mood of England. The Henley Regatta, cricket test matches, soccer finals, the Chelsea Flower Show. These things seem to be as important to the English as a general election. How the weather will affect the cricket and tennis is as important as how it will affect the harvest.

There is a different feeling in London during the fortnight in June when the grass-court tennis championships are played in Wimbledon. Visitors flock to London to watch the game. Wimbledon happens during the two weeks when strawberries are at their best. Strawberries with cream is the favorite refreshment of the spectators. I quite enjoy waiting for them to finish their strawberry picnics: Slimming humans sometimes leave cream on their plates on the grass, which is nice for me.

THE OPERA AT GLYNDEBOURNE IS ANOTHER summer excitement. The house, theater, and gardens are set in the rolling Sussex Downs. The theater was built in the 1930s by John Christie for his wife, singer Audrey Mildmay. Five or six operas are performed every year. The performances start in the late afternoon: During the long interval the audience can have dinner in the restaurant, or picnic in the garden. The audience all wear evening dress. I prefer the picnics because I can join in. I also like the intervals best and so, I have heard, do some of the audience.

THE GROWTH OF THE SUPERMARKETS and the ease of going shopping by car have closed many small village shops. Until well into the 1950s, every village used to have its own post office, butcher, baker, and general store. But now it is very unusual to find a single shop in small villages in most parts of the country. This is particularly true of the villages within easy access of larger towns. In remote parts of the country, like parts of Cornwall and Yorkshire, there are still some village shops. I don't remember the days when every village had its own small grocer and general store, but I am told that cats used to sit in the windows among the cakes, buns, and sweets, and listen to the village people coming in for a gossip. That wouldn't be considered hygienic now. Some village shops that used to sell food now sell antiques. But this butcher's shop is just pretending to be an antique shop.

DIFFERENT AREAS OF THE COUNTRY seem to have adopted different color schemes. Many of the seaside houses in Cornwall are whitewashed, with ultramarine or cobalt-blue paintwork. It is odd to see houses in Sussex and Hampshire that are pink, but they seem to fit in in East Anglia as well as they do in the South of France. I have noticed recently, particularly in East Anglia, that people are painting the outsides of their houses in very vivid colors and with no reference to the color of their next door neighbor's house.

Houses close to the sea are often painted very brightly—especially on the Suffolk coast. Seaside architecture lends itself to jolly painting. Maybe the buildings have to compete with the colors of beach clothes and windsurfers' sails. Color choices are so influenced by fashion, there is natural desire for change.

FRESH FISH
SHELL FISH
Daily
CRABS
LOBSTER

53

ONE HARDLY EVER SEES A YELLOW CAR in England these days—although I'm told that at one time there were many. However, it is no surprise to find one on the Cowdray Estate on the edge of Midhurst. Everything that has anything to do with Lord Cowdray is painted a hot yellow. The color looks amazing with the local brick and tile work. The buildings, painted yellow and carefully looked after by the landlord, stretch for at least ten miles around Midhurst.

The estate yard at the edge of the town, where all the repair work is carried out, has some very attractive buildings. It is a good cat's playground. There is a footpath that goes up to Cowdray House. Pheasants often cross my path here.

Eating and drinking well are very important while traveling. There is always a moment just before twelve-thirty when we think we ought to be looking for a pub: Although I always heartily agree and say so, it does seem a little greedy to want to eat so early. We go past an attractive-looking pub just because it is rude to look too eager, and then no other pub looks nice for miles, or a car is coming too quickly behind us and we miss an opportunity to stop. We go on, and by the time we find a pub that looks nice, lunch is no longer being served.

Although the licensing laws have changed in England and pubs are allowed to stay open all day, few do, and fewer still serve food all day. Pubs, and fish-and-chip shops, are still the best and cheapest places to eat when touring Britain. I like a pub with a good name. Lions often give their names to pubs; hence the number of Red Lion, Black Lion, or White Lion pubs.

The Red Lion at Chalton is a good pub to visit. There is a fine place to sit outside on a grassy bank across the road. They serve country wines made of elderflowers and gooseberries. I'm quite happy with any scraps of food I can get.

ALDEBURGH IS A TOWN FULL OF HOUSES with names to make one's mouth water: Shrimp Cottage, The Gulls, Herrings Restaurant. Before Benjamin Britten started his music festival in 1948, Aldeburgh was just a small fishing town, but now it is internationally famous. A lot of Britten's work is directly inspired by Aldeburgh and the sea.

The real attraction for cats and fish-loving humans is the sheds and boats along the seashore. The daily catch of sole, plaice, cod, herring, and fresh crab and lobster is sold from sheds. Maybe some of the fish goes to the wonderful fish-and-chip shop on the corner of Crabbe Street.

MANY PEOPLE CLAIM THEIR TOWN has the best
fish-and-chip shop in the country. I always like to eat fish and
chips in Aldeburgh. Not far away, farther inland, is a small town
called Eye. The fish-and-chip shop there also has delicious food. There
are fish-and-chip shops all over the country, but the best ones
are near the coast. Even though you
can now take home almost any
cooked food you could name,
there is something very cozy
and English about a
"fish supper."

It used to be served in real newspaper, but the health authorities decided printing ink was not good for you. So now fish-and-chip suppers are packed in plain newsprint paper with no writing on it.

THAXTED HAS SOME OF THE PRETTIEST ARCHITECTURE in Essex. Many of the medieval Essex towns throve on the wool trade, but Thaxted's prosperity came from the manufacture of knives and swords. The Guildhall was built by the cutlers of Thaxted in 1475. The ground floor is open to the street and a good place for cats to play. The old wooden beams would be nice for sharpening my claws, but I think there would be real trouble if I even touched them.

Not far from the Guildhall, near the church, are the charming Almshouses. Almost dollhouse size. Do all old people really get small enough for these houses? I think they are more suitable for a cat.

THE LAND IN SUFFOLK IS VERY FERTILE, flat, and windy, so there are quite a lot of windmills in Suffolk. There has been a windmill on this site since 1287. The present building dates from 1796.

Saxtead Green Mill produced flour until the Second World War. During the war it had to grind corn for animal food and never went back to making flour.

I wish I could have visited this windmill
when it was working. I imagine I might have
found quite a lot of mice around.
It is now in the guardianship of
English Heritage, and open to the public. Mice are scarce.

THE SMALL WOOL TOWNS AND VILLAGES of the Suffolk–East Borders are among the most unspoiled in England. My favorite is Lavenham. It seems to be just as it was when it was built, in the fifteenth and sixteenth centuries. Many of the houses are quite crooked and sagging with age, but all are wonderfully preserved.

The wood on the half-timbered houses is left unpainted and has
shades of silver gray and pale brown. The plasterwork between the
timbers is painted in pinks and terra-cottas. I like to think of Lavenham
as a tabby town: The stripes formed by the vertical timbers remind me of
the coats on some of my striped friends.

QUITE NEAR CAMBRIDGE IS WIMPOLE HALL, a spectacular eighteenth-century house with a lovely collection of furniture. There are a well-restored Victorian stable block, some heavy horses, and a huge park. I like to run in the green fields—avoiding the sheep of course—and rest under the great shady trees.

At the side of the park is Wimpole Home Farm, which is my favorite part of the estate to visit, although extra animals are not too welcome. This has been a working farm since the eighteenth century and was one of the most important places for progressive farming in England. Huge thatched barns surround the clean farmyard with nicely fenced

enclosures where the animals munch straw all day. I wouldn't mind spending an odd night in one of these barns.

The Great Barn was designed by Sir John Soane, who was also involved in the design of Wimpole Hall itself. The Great Barn has recently been restored by the National Trust. The farm buildings around the Great Barn contain a collection of brightly colored carts. Most important is the collection of rare breeds of farm livestock. There are many varieties of cows, sheep, and goats, a large Tamworth pig, and best of all, rare breeds of chickens. I love chickens. There are so many shapes, sizes, and markings to be found among the old breeds, and although some of these hens don't lay as well as the more modern crossbred hens, their eggs are lovely. The very dark brown eggs that the Moran lays are shiny and sometimes speckled; the Arucana's eggs are pale blue.

At THE BACK OF THE RABBIT ENCLOSURES there is a Victorian Gothic dairy (shaped like a cottage), which was built in 1862. Inside it is lined with cool tiles bordered with ivy patterns. There are big cream dishes and butter churns and other equipment connected with dairy products. There are several notices warning humans not to touch anything. I wish someone there would make a little cream or swing a muslin bag of curd and drip whey into a bowl. I wish I could take home some brown Moran eggs to admire and then eat.

Two of the most beautiful towns in England are
Cambridge and Oxford. Both are university towns. Both have a great
deal of medieval architecture. Both are made for walking or cycling.
Motorcars are really unwelcome.

Cambridge is dedicated almost entirely to the university. The nicest thing about visiting the university buildings is going through the tall archways into the courtyards of bright green grass. Cambridge, naturally, is full of busy young people clutching books, cycling, and chattering.

On Christmas Eve the whole country listens to the King's College choirboys singing carols. In summer it is nice to walk along the Backs and stroll down the college gardens to the river Cam. I like to hop into a bicycle basket and have a ride around the town.

ALTHOUGH IT IS SURROUNDED BY busy industrial suburbs, Oxford is as beautiful as Cambridge. The views behind the college gateways are just as lovely and serene.

The river Isis runs through the water meadows. Blackwell's, the famous bookshop, is on Broad Street. And the Ashmolean is always good to visit.

University College claims to be the oldest college in Oxford, and has naturally had its share of famous graduates. University College men have founded industries, played international cricket, run newspapers, and become famous theater directors. But only one has become president of the United States, and he has the most famous cat in the world: Socks.

LOOKING ROUND GARDENS IS, without doubt, one of my greatest pleasures. It is all so easy: The car is parked in a tidy car park, and for an hour or two you are free to believe the garden is yours. There are amazing displays of wild and eccentric topiary at Levens Hall (Cumbria) and Packwood (Warwickshire). Neat and formal topiary can be found at Lanhydrock (Cornwall), Montacute House (Somerset), and Blickling Hall (Norfolk). I love greenhouses too: from the wonderful Palm House at Kew to the smallest glass house for rearing seedlings. Best of all I like to see a formal herb garden or a well-kept kitchen garden. The herbs and roses planted among the box hedges are a nice surprise at the Museum of Garden History at Lambeth. And there is a good kitchen garden at Fenton House in London.

On some days of the year, proud gardeners open their private gardens to the public, charging a small fee, which is always for charity. Some of the private gardens are quite as grand as the well-known national ones, and some are very small.

Quite, quite different from anywhere is the wonderful garden at Stourhead in Wiltshire [see the next page]. As you enter the garden from the village of Stourton you go straight into a most magical world. Whichever direction you take, there are breathtaking views, which change around every corner.

I LIKE TO GO TO DEVON IN THE SPRINGTIME. The very
narrow lanes are covered with flowers: tall foxgloves, buttercups, blue-
bells, wild strawberries, and pink campion, all out at the same time.

80

It is like walking down a corridor papered with very richly flowered
wallpaper. And what glorious smells: wild garlic and bluebell mixed
with rabbit, mouse, and vole.

THE PILCHARD IS A FOURTEENTH-CENTURY PUB
that used to be frequented by smugglers. I was attracted
by the name. I can think of easier places to visit,
but it is quite exciting having to get across the
water on a motorized bus on stilts. When the tide
is low, you can walk across the beach. But the
bus runs very frequently, so there is no fear of
getting stuck on the island. Inside, the pub is
friendly and cozy. Sometimes I manage to
get some mackerel, but seldom pilchards,
I'm afraid.

HOUSES AND GARDENS THAT ARE OPEN to the public quite often have notices saying NO DOGS ALLOWED or DOGS ON LEADS ONLY, or have a picture of a dog with a line going through it. There is almost never a sign saying NO CATS ALLOWED, so I take this as an invitation to enter any house I please. Certainly I feel Knightshayes must be a place for cats. Set in its massive wooden front door is a cat flap.

The house was designed by William Burges in 1870. Its elaborate Victorian interior has many chairs perfect for naps. The highlight of the garden is the topiary hedge depicting a hunting scene.

I WOULD VERY MUCH LIKE TO GET INSIDE some of these country houses—especially inside the kitchens. Because no one lives in them, however, there is probably not much cooking going on: no scraps of food to attract mice, no milk to drink, no warm stoves to sleep by. I did manage to slip into the kitchen at Lanhydrock. The kitchen is enormous and very austere. There is a nice collection of pans, pots, and jelly molds.

I was very surprised to see another cat at Lanhydrock. We played on the dresser for a while. When the smell of copper polish became overwhelming, we left.

The house was built in the seventeenth century and rebuilt after a fire in 1881. Run by the National Trust, it is one of the most popular places to visit in Cornwall. The original seventeenth-century gatehouse and north wing remain. The plasterwork in the Great Gallery is very ornate. I like playing in the huge wooded park or jumping around in the formal garden.

MOUSEHOLE IS A PRETTY VILLAGE with a harbor full of fishing boats and gulls. The streets are very narrow, and nearly every white-washed cottage looks like a good place for a cat to live. In fact, I am told the cat population of Cornwall is one of the highest in England. Whenever we drive around, the sea seems to be everywhere. This means a plentiful supply of fish. There are many other good things to eat in Cornwall: The ice cream is delicious; there are Cornish pasties and (the great specialty) cream teas. A pot of tea, scones, jam, and clotted cream are the essential ingredients for a cream tea. You don't put the cream in the tea, you put it on the scone with the jam. Cream teas are served at all kinds of places: country houses, farms, pubs, as well as cafés specially dedicated to them. One of the best is Annie's in Mousehole.

I OFTEN GO TO ST. ENODOC [see the previous page], a kind of pilgrimage to visit John Betjeman's grave. The perfect small church where he is buried was once completely covered by sand. John Betjeman loved Cornwall and lived there for long periods of his life.

I seem to spend quite a lot of my time visiting churches. I often call in at a wedding on a Saturday afternoon, even if I'm not invited. I may find a church mouse or two to chase. And I like to listen to the hymns and look at people's clothes.

The regular services in country churches are best of all. I am very keen on tombs, especially ones with carved marble figures on top. But my favorite thing is poking around behind the pews to see what kind of designs the kneelers have.

There are some very good ones at St. Enodoc, many depicting cheerful birds and lively fishes. The best designs of all are on the kneelers in a church at Steep in Hampshire. They were designed by the Canon Douglas Snelgar and made by the parishioners. There are doves and kingfishers, robins and swallows, fish and hedgehogs, and lots of flowers. I get so disappointed when I find a church with plain blue leather ones.

It is a good idea to go where birds go. You can't go wrong if you follow the gulls. I followed them to Cadgwith Cove down at the very south tip of Cornwall [see the next page]. This is one of the most picturesque little fishing villages in England.

The Cadgwith Cove fishermen chop up fish heads and scraps for bait, and the gulls swoop down to get the scraps. I hope to get some too.

ONE THING I HAVE NOTICED: There are very few toy cats about;
there are many more toy bears. I suppose most children grow up with a
toy bear and a real cat. I don't expect many families could cope with real
bears. Small children often treat cats as toys; I wish they wouldn't.

There is nothing more nostalgic than your own childhood. I remember my kittenhood with great affection. I was picked up and cuddled much more than I am now. I had very appetizing food and loved all my brothers and sisters. I am told they all went to excellent homes. I don't think I'd recognize them if I saw them, but as I wander about, looking at the delights of England, I do feel there are certain cats with whom I have more in common than others.

Parents are so anxious to keep their children from breaking their best toys that dolls are often locked away and kept in tissue. I suspect this is why so many beautiful doll collections exist. The Bethnal Green Museum in South East London has one of the best collections of dolls, dollhouses, and toys. But there are countless other collections throughout the country. Driving south from Yorkshire on the A1 we saw a tantalizing sign "DOLL MUSEUM" very close to the motorway. This particular museum has a stunning collection of old dolls, toys, prams, and childhood memorabilia. It also has some elaborate contemporary dolls in the likenesses of the Royal Family, the Beatles, and Elvis Presley. The rooms are all stuffed with dolls. The entrance fee was a modest £1.50 for humans; I managed to slip in without paying.

I DO LIKE A GOOD EARTHENWARE SAUCER or plate for my milk and food. I always think plastic, paper, and tin make the food taste different. We have a lot of earthenware and china in the house. It is a nice thing to collect: not as bulky as furniture and very decorative. I have my favorite saucers, of course, but I'm not often given the really good ones.

It is interesting to go to the town where pottery is made. Stoke-on-Trent is still a very busy industrial town, and I love seeing the skyline of kilns and chimneys as we turn off the motorway. The towns immortalized by Arnold Bennett's *Anna of the Five Towns* make up Stoke-on-Trent. Actually, there are six: Burslem, Hanley, Stoke, Longton, Fenton, and Tunstall.

Many of the factories still produce wares under the name of the family that started them, such as Minton, Doulton, Mason, Copeland, and Wedgwood. There is a statue of Josiah Wedgwood outside the station as you enter the Potteries. Some of the factories are still on their original sites along the Trent and Mersey canals. The pottery was transported by canal until the railway and road transport took over.

Some of the important long-established potteries (like Spode, Coalport, and Minton) have museums, where pieces dating from the eighteenth century through to the present day are shown. And the Wedgwood Visitor Centre just outside Stoke at Barlaston is worth a visit.

Sᴛᴏᴋᴇ-ᴏɴ-Tʀᴇɴᴛ's Cɪᴛʏ Mᴜsᴇᴜᴍ is in Hanley; it houses a comprehensive collection of ceramic art from tiles and tableware to figurines, huge urns, and large ceramic sculptures.

There is a good collection of Staffordshire figurines in the museum, and shelves and shelves of the cow-shaped jugs known as creamers— the tail is the handle, the mouth is the spout, and there is a little lid on the back. The museum also has painting, sculpture, and costume galleries.

Just outside Stoke-on-Trent is a garden called Biddulph Grange, which was recently taken over by the National Trust. It is an early Victorian garden and has some very unusual features: There are some Egyptian sphinxes, clipped yew hedges, and a Chinese garden with a red lacquer bridge.

THE COUNTRYSIDE AROUND STOKE-ON-TRENT is very dramatic. Driving into Cheshire, Derbyshire, Lancashire, or farther north is a temptation, but we took a turning on the right just fifteen miles or so out of Stoke-on-Trent and came upon a small market town called Longnor. I went to the church first, as usual. The church was rather a distinguished-looking eighteenth-century building with a nice graveyard on the side of a hill.

I was astounded to find the sign PLEASE CLOSE THE INNER DOOR BECAUSE CATS ENTER. This is the first time I have been made to feel so unwelcome.

I felt more welcome when I went for a little walk behind the church and found a house with a back garden teeming with chickens, goats, rabbits, and mandarin ducks. The three marmalade and two tabby cats were extremely friendly. We intend to keep in touch.

When we go down country roads that are unfamiliar to me, I think of the local cats who know every smell, every blade of grass, where the best mice live, and where the blackbirds make their nests, and I wonder what it would be like to live there. Humans are always saying, "If only I had

another life I'd like to live here." Of course they don't, but I do. I don't feel I've had eight lives yet. In my next one, this is where I would like to live: a small house in Crayke. Or maybe on this farm in the next village, Bransby, on the way to Helmsley.

It doesn't matter where we drive in Yorkshire—everything is beautiful. Maybe because it is always sunny when we visit. The green hedges are shiny and well trimmed, the grass is luscious, and the pheasants are fat and colorful. The hedges are quite low so one can see

beautiful landscapes almost continuously. Well-kept farms, healthy flocks of sheep, and herds of cows rush by.

Because this area is so beautiful, we just drive where we will. We never follow a sign until we come to the one that points to Helmsley, and we take it.

H ELMSLEY
is quite a big market
town in a prosperous part of North
Yorkshire. The square, with its magnificent market cross, is
lined with pretty houses, shops, and hotels. The White Swan is a fine
place to stay. Usually I stay in the car. Wandering off the square you'll

find horses in stables, blacksmiths, a gunsmith, and shops that sell delicious pies. Yorkshire is famous for its pies and puddings.

THE MOORS ARE MADE FOR QUIET MOTORING. Because there are sheep crossing the road every few minutes, no one drives very fast and there is time to slow down and look at every breathtaking view. The floors of the valley are a rich green; sheep and cows appear as tiny specks in the distance. It is wonderful to play in the heather and bracken. Almost as soon as I jump from the car and walk a few yards down the bracken and heather slopes, the road, traffic, and people are gone and I am alone in miles of moorland.

Hard as it may be to believe, the sea is very near the Yorkshire moors. In fact, no spot in England is ever more than seventy miles away from the sea.

One of the best sights in North Yorkshire is on the northeast coast in a town called Whitby. The ruined abbey and church sit high on a cliff above the sea, the boats, and the old town [see the next page]. Pevsner called the abbey: "One of the most moving ruins in England."

I LIKE TO CLIMB THE 199 STEPS to visit the church and abbey. I am told that there are witches in Whitby. I have often wondered how a cat could fly with a witch on a broomstick. And why.

S CARBOROUGH HAS BEEN A POPULAR COASTAL RESORT
since the late eighteenth century. (Sheridan's *Trip to Scarborough* was
written in 1777.) The cliffs are very high, and there are
funicular railways going through the garden walks
to take people down to the beach. I prefer running
down the zigzag paths. But I am extremely careful
along the Esplanade. The sea can get very rough;
the humans driving by often have to keep their
car windows firmly closed as the waves crash
along the sea road. The town itself is full of
magnificent buildings. The Grand Hotel, designed
by Cuthbert Broderick, is particularly handsome and towers above the
north cliff. Scarborough's theater is famous as the home of Alan
Ayckbourn's plays. The town itself is full of attractions, including
Peasholm Park and Oliver's Mount. Down by the seashore there is the
delicious, familiar smell of cockles,
winkles, mussels, and fried fish.
There is an outdoor fun fair in
addition to the usual seaside
attractions: fortune-tellers, silly
hats, tattooing booths, and
buckets and spades and balls
with which to play on
the beach.

And you can buy Scarborough rock, a long, sticky sugar stick with the name of the town running through it.

I REFUSE TO GO ON FISHING TRIPS in the North Sea; it is much too rough and I get sick on boats. But I like to visit Filey and Bridlington, fishing towns with sandy beaches. After I have had enough sea, I come inland a little to Beverley, a smallish market town boasting two very impressive churches. The Minster is bigger and better known, but I also like to take a look at St. Mary's when I visit. Beverley was a walled town. Almost all the walls have gone, but a gateway, North Bar, remains, and divides the town into two areas: North Bar Within and North Bar Without. The two churches and the market cross are Within.

Without the North Bar is Beverley Westwood, a pleasant place for picnics and home to countless rabbits.

WHILE EXPLORING THE OLD PART OF HULL, just by the house where William Wilberforce used to live, I looked down and noticed, set into the pavement, a silvery fish, then another, then a whole shoal of tiny fish. I thought they looked very nice. I was surprised to find that all over this area there are low relief sculptures in metal and stone representing the fishes traditionally landed in Hull. The sculptures, by Gordon Young, were commissioned in 1992 and form an alphabet, from Anchovy to Zander. They are all in the old part of Hull, where the docks used to be. If London's streets are paved with gold, Hull's are paved with fish.

Harrogate's streets are bordered with flowers. All over the town, in the parks and on the roundabouts, there are flower beds. It was a fashionable resort at the beginning of this century, and humans would come to "take the waters." Hence the huge Edwardian

hotels, lovely places to stay when driving around in North Yorkshire.
Harrogate is also home to Betty's Tea Shop: Humans feast on
delicious bacon and egg breakfasts; I prefer a lick of cream from
Betty's teatime cakes.

I LOVE MOTORING THE WAY WE DO IT. There is something intensely satisfying about being shut up in a glass and metal box. One can look out happily at frosty fields and feel snug and smug, or enjoy a breeze from the open window on a warm sunny day. We arrive and leave when we want, and stop when we want. We never have to think of timetables.

We can fill the back of the car with stones, seashells, seaweed, an antique we found in a little shop somewhere, fruit, eggs, cream, and honey bought at the roadside. There may even be time for me to paint a quick watercolor out of the side window. If I can keep my paws warm.

*A Note About the Author*

Pat Albeck is a long-established and prolific artist,
who creates brilliant designs for fabric, ceramics, tea towels,
tins and boxes for the National Trust and department stores
and museums shops throughout the world.
She lives by the river Thames in Hammersmith, London.
She is married to theatre designer Peter Rice
and her son is designer Matthew Rice.

The State Bed in the Queen Anne room at Dyrham Park, Gloucestershire